Where Do Babies Come From?

*B. W.—To my wonderful parents, Ray T. and Val C. Wilcox.
Thanks for everything!*

*B. C.—To my wife, Michelle, who has always stood by me and helped me
in my career as an artist; and to our son Kyle, who was born in the
middle of this project and turned out to be the perfect model. Special thanks
to Shauna Gibby for giving me the opportunity to illustrate this book.*

Text © 2004 Brad Wilcox

Illustrations © 2004 Brian Call

Visit us at deseretbook.com

Library of Congress Cataloging-in-Publication Data

    Wilcox, Brad.
        Where do babies come from? / Brad Wilcox ; illustrations by Brian D. Call.
        p.   cm.
        ISBN 1-59038-237-4 (pbk.)
        1. Sex instruction for children—Religious aspects—Mormon Church.   I. Call, Brian D.   II. Title.
        HQ57.W568 2004
        241'.66—dc22   2003024683

Printed in China   18961
R. R. Donnelley and Sons, Shenzen

10   9   8   7   6   5   4   3   2

Where Do Babies Come From?

Brad Wilcox
Illustrated by Brian Call

DESERET
BOOK

SALT LAKE CITY, UTAH

Acknowledgments

Thanks to my youngest children, Whitney and David, for being my main editors on this project. I also appreciate John and Kim Bytheway for their support. Because their children are arriving at the ages when this book might be helpful, their interest was especially encouraging. Thanks to Emily Watts, who never gave up on this project and saw it through even after I left on my mission to Chile. The illustrations and design have enriched the original manuscript greatly. I appreciate Brian Call, Shauna Gibby, and Janna DeVore, along with the entire staff at Deseret Book. Finally, I owe so much to my wife, Debi—not only for her input on this book, but also for her help and support in all I do. Thanks for giving birth to our own four children and caring for our family so masterfully.

Preface

Since the publication of *Growing Up: Gospel Answers about Maturation and Sex,* I have received many requests for a similar book for younger children that could serve as an introduction to sexuality. One mother said, "There are already lots of books and videos available to parents but nothing that addresses this topic from an LDS perspective." I had presumed that an LDS perspective wasn't necessary at such a basic level. Still, at the insistent encouragement of this mother I began to review the offerings of a variety of publishers, including books on the Christian market. I also reviewed a few previous Deseret Book publications that are no longer in print.

It didn't take long for me to conclude that there really was a need for an introductory volume for young children that is simple and straightforward without being crass, crude, or silly. Even the religious books, while sensitive, seemed to be missing something by not presenting procreation in the context of the plan of salvation. I determined to add this book to the list of resources available for helping parents with the sometimes-overwhelming responsibility of teaching children about sex.

In this book, general teaching guidelines for parents are presented at the beginning, while the main text and illustrations are appropriate for parents to read with younger children. The questions and answers at the end of the book would be best read and discussed only with older children. It is hoped that adults will be selective in an effort to meet individual needs of young family members.

Teaching Children about Sexuality

President David O. McKay would never do that! That was the first thought I had when I learned how babies are conceived. Obviously, I was wrong. President McKay had a strong marriage and a wonderful family. My own children had similar responses when I first spoke to each of them in turn. *Gross, sick,* and *disgusting* were a few words I remember hearing. Such responses underscore the need for parents to provide not only the facts but also the perspective that will help children be able to adjust their thinking and see sex as a valuable and positive part of marriage and a vital element in the creation of eternal families.

Regarding parental duty to teach children about sexuality, the First Presidency has said, "This responsibility cannot wisely be left to society, nor the schools: nor can the responsibility be shifted to the Church. It is the responsibility of parents to see that they fully perform their duty in this respect" (in Conference Report, April 1969, 13). It is in the home that facts and values can be combined and presented with balance. Parents are best qualified to teach about topics that are personal and sacred because they have a unique concern for their children's welfare, choices, and futures unequaled elsewhere. As we take this responsibility, we will share moments with our children that can build trust and security and strengthen bonds between us. Still, sex can seem an intimidating topic.

Some parents worry that by speaking frankly with children about their bodies and sexuality they are somehow promoting or condoning promiscuous behavior. My experience has taught me the opposite is true. The most sexually active teens I have encountered are usually the least informed. It is silence and ignorance, not open communication, which often lead to poor choices. The more solid sexual information children receive from their parents, the more capable they are of making righteous and mature choices. In fact, some studies indicate that parents who talk with their children about sex actually delay their children's sexual involvement because they satisfy curiosity that so often leads to experimentation.

Other parents feel insecure because they think they don't know enough. You don't have to be a medical doctor to explain great-grandma's stroke to a child or a biologist to answer questions about how plants grow. While we may not feel like experts on the topic of sex, we certainly know more than talkative boys on the playground. We obviously understand rights, risks, and responsibilities associated with sex a lot better than the writers of most TV shows. We know more than we think we do.

Seven key words—all starting with *p*—can guide us as we approach the subject: *process, personalize, private, probing, point blank, positive,* and *perspective.*

Teaching is a process. A lot of people think sex education consists of sitting down with a child and having "the talk" or passing them a book like this one and saying, "Here, read this." While talks and books are helpful, perhaps the greatest purpose they serve is to open doors of communication between parents and children. Sex education needs to be a continuous flow of information through every age and stage as we attempt to meet the individual needs and circumstances of each child. "The talk" is not the end. It is just one more ongoing step along the way.

Personalize the experience. Children love to hear the story of their own births. Tell your son about the anxiety you felt when you discovered the umbilical cord had become wrapped around his neck and the relief you felt when you found it had not caused any damage. Tell your daughter about the first time you heard her heart beating or how she was so "modest" during the ultrasound that you couldn't tell at first if she was a boy or girl. Tell your children of the prayers and blessings prior to the birth, the tears of gratitude that came after. These personalized stories provide a natural, comfortable, and incredibly meaningful context for learning more about procreation. Without such a context, the process can sound too dehumanized and distant. As we personalize our teaching we help children sense the wonder and joy associated with the miracle of creation.

Speak in private. Privacy may help us avoid feelings of awkwardness. Even family home evening may be too public a setting to meet the needs of everyone gathered without embarrassing some and overwhelming others. Personal conversations allow us to teach more sensitively and effectively. One woman remembers how awkward it was when her parents once taught some facts of life in family home evening. She and her twin brother were very curious, asking all sorts of questions, while her older brother and sister were mortified and her younger siblings were clueless.

Ask probing questions. Once we are in private, asking probing questions will help us know when not to overload children with more information than they really need or want. I love the classic tale of the overanxious mother whose six-year-old asked, "Where did I come from?" The mother took a deep breath and launched into a facts-of-life oration. Finally, the little girl interrupted, "Mom, all I was wondering was where I came from. My friend Stephanie says she came from Omaha." The surest way to estimate just how much children know or want to know is by probing. For example, as a child asks, "Why aren't my breasts as big as mommy's" or "Where do babies come from?" A parent might reply, "What made you think of that?" Another child asks, "What does adultery mean?" The parent may respond, "What do you think it means?" Probing questions are not an attempt to change the subject or avoid giving a straight answer. Rather, they offer a chance to listen as well as speak—to gather enough information to respond effectively.

Offer point-blank information. When we have determined what a child knows and what we need to teach, we must not hesitate to offer point-blank information. We need to be factual, honest, and direct, even if we feel uneasy. If you don't know an answer, it's okay to say, "You know, I'm not quite sure about that. Let's find out together." Willingness to talk to our children truthfully, despite uneasiness, will strengthen our children's confidence in us. While frankness is important in all the answers we provide, we should use proper vocabulary instead of gutter or slang terms in our discussions. Such terms communicate irreverence for a sacred topic. It may take a little effort on our part, but we can become comfortable calling body functions and parts by their proper names.

Be positive about the subject. Information about sex doesn't have to be discussed grimly or solemnly. A light and positive touch can make discussion easier. Too often we unintentionally convey negative messages about our children's bodies by our tone or word choice. We teach object lessons by chewing up gum or crushing flowers and then saying, "If you have sex, this is you." One Latter-day Saint sixth grader asked his teacher about AIDS. The teacher said, "I'd love to talk to you about that, but first go home and ask your dad." The boy said, "I did, but all he said was that AIDS had to do with sex so I wasn't supposed to worry about it." Then this sixth grader asked, "So, what about sex?" His father responded, "Sex is the second worst sin next to murder." The father probably intended to communicate that adultery and fornication are grievous sins. However, consider the message this boy received instead. Of course children need to be warned about the consequences of immorality, but we must also acknowledge that sex within marriage serves wonderful and important purposes.

Discuss sexuality from a gospel perspective. Along with being positive, we always need to discuss sexuality within a gospel perspective. A lot of books address the topic of sexuality for children and young people, but not in the context of Latter-day Saint values, doctrines, and standards. Many books describe sex in ways that are incompatible with our Heavenly Father's plan for our happiness. Spiritual things and sexual things are not opposites. Within the bounds the Lord has set, they complement each other. They can strengthen each other and coexist beautifully. How grateful we can be for the standards, guidance, and perspective the gospel provides. We don't just have rules, we have reasons to keep them.

Long before we came to earth we lived with Heavenly Father and Heavenly Mother, the parents of our spirits. They loved us and we loved them. We wanted to become just like them because they were so wonderful. We saw they had perfected bodies of flesh and bone and knew that if we were ever to be like our heavenly parents we would need physical bodies also. Heavenly Father presented a plan that would allow us to come to earth and, among other things, get bodies. We shouted for joy.

Moms and dads help Heavenly Father provide bodies for his spirit children. Inside the private parts of a father and mother are tiny cells, like seeds, that can make a baby's body. Dad's cells are called sperm and Mom's cells are called eggs. The eggs don't have a hard shell and are not big like the eggs you know. Mom's egg cells are smaller than grains of salt. Dad's sperm cells are even smaller. They can be seen only with microscopes.

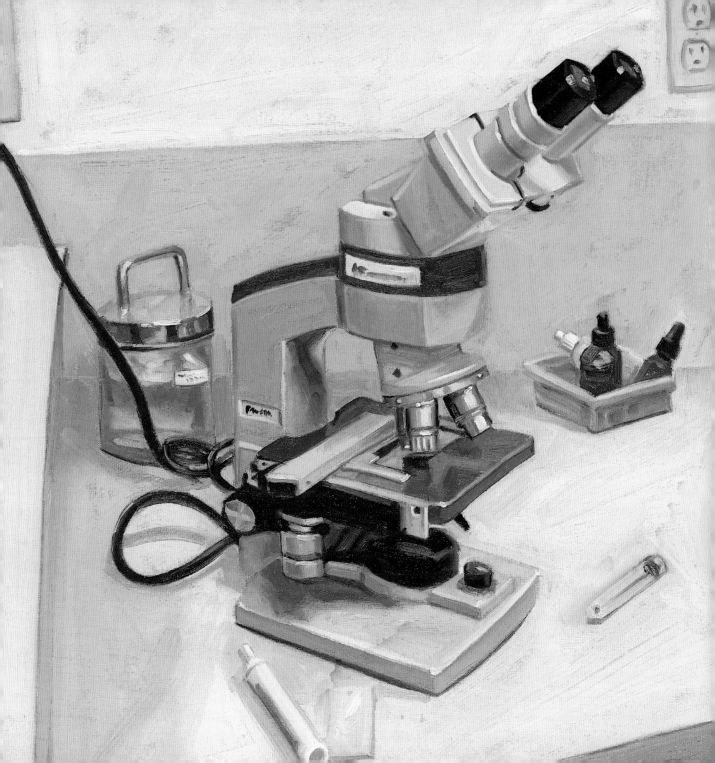

It takes both a dad and a mom to make a baby. Neither one can do it alone. Dad's sperm cell has part of the instructions and Mom's egg cell has the other part—like two parts of a treasure map. Only together do they have all the information needed to create the treasure, the marvelous human body Heavenly Father sent us to earth to get—a physical body made in his image. When Dad's sperm cell joins with Mom's egg cell, a baby's body begins to develop.

When the baby starts to grow, we say Mom is pregnant.

It takes nine months for the baby to finish growing inside of her.

Mom's middle gets bigger and bigger. She sometimes feels tired

because it is hard work preparing for a baby, but she and Dad are

happy that Heavenly Father is sending a baby for them to love

and care for.

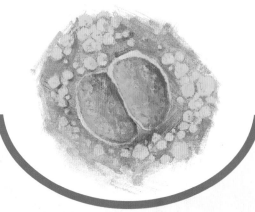

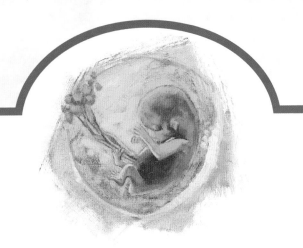

When you were inside your mom you could hear her voice and her heart beating. You moved around and your mom could feel you moving. Sometimes your dad would put his hand on Mom's middle and you would push against his hand. No one could see you because you were inside of your mother; but you slept, woke, smiled, yawned, hiccuped, and even sucked your thumb.

Inside your mother you got food and oxygen through a flexible tube that connected your body with hers. It is called the umbilical cord. It was snipped off when you were born. Don't worry. It didn't hurt. Your belly button is where the umbilical cord once was.

When your parents visited the doctor while they were expecting you, they got to listen to your heart beat. It sounded like a fast swishing noise. Even though they hadn't seen you yet, your parents loved you and spent a lot of time wondering what you would be like. They dreamed of the wonderful things they would do with you. They knew you would not remember your time with Heavenly Father and Heavenly Mother. They knew it would be up to them to teach you about God and Jesus and why you are here on earth.

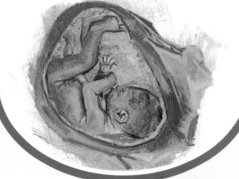

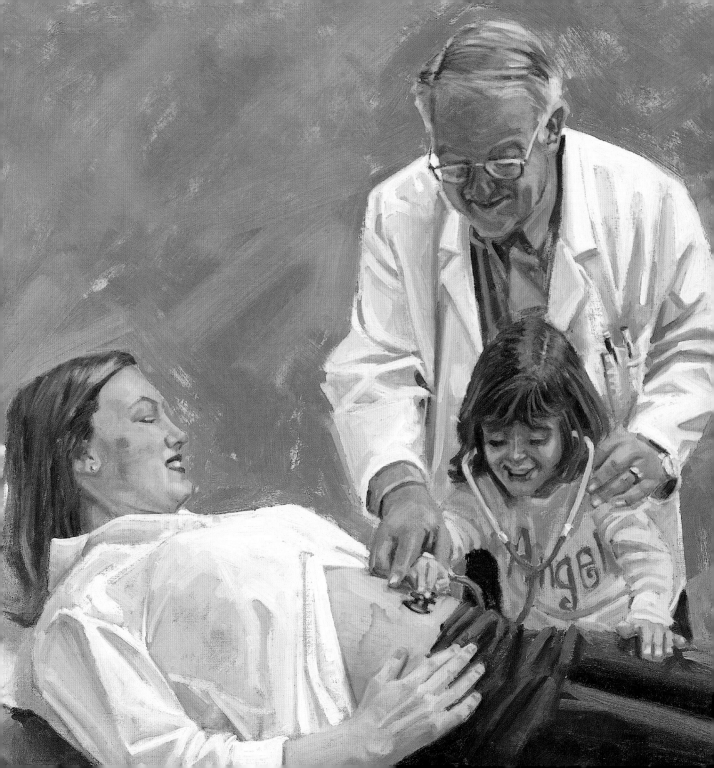

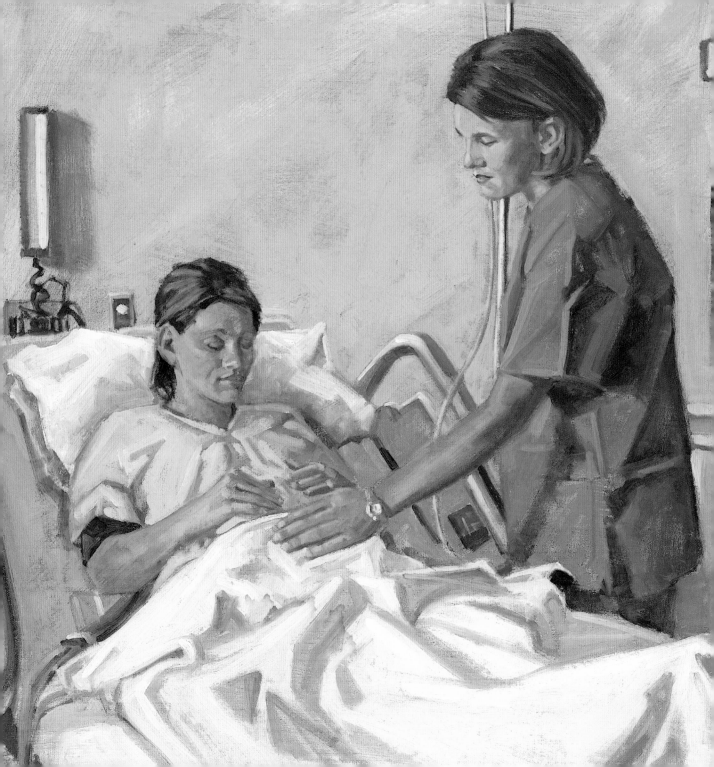

Most moms go to the hospital to have their babies, but it's not because they are sick. It's just a safe, clean place where doctors and nurses can help make sure moms and babies are okay. When it's time for the baby to be born, Mom's muscles around her middle will tighten and then relax over and over. This pushes the baby out of Mom's body through her vagina between her legs. The vagina can stretch until it's big enough for the baby to come out, but it's still a tight squeeze, and it's hard work for Mom. That's why they call it labor. Having a baby is tiring and painful, but it's worth it. Moms are willing to go through a lot because they love their babies.

Dad's job during your birth was to help and support your mom and you. He prayed for you both and may have given Mom a priesthood blessing. He appreciated her for all she was going through. When you finally came out, took your first breath of air, and let out a cry, both your dad and your mom were relieved and happy. They held you in their arms, stroked your skin, and whispered how much they loved you.

Along with being able to have babies, moms' bodies also can feed babies. Moms' breasts produce milk. When babies get hungry they don't start off eating food the way grown-ups do. They drink milk from their mothers' breasts or from a baby bottle. The milk gives babies all the energy they need to keep growing.

Babies are born into families, and families are very important. Babies need moms, dads, brothers, sisters, grandmas, and grandpas to help them. They can't do a lot on their own yet. They need to be washed, held, read to, kissed, cuddled, and loved.

Babies don't stay babies for long. They are constantly growing. They learn to laugh, play, crawl, walk, and talk. They learn about Heavenly Father and Jesus and how they once lived with them. They learn about all they must do to return home to live with them again. They have lots of questions about why the sun shines and how animals talk to each other. They will even get old enough to begin to wonder how babies are born, just as you have.

Some people think that life begins when Dad's sperm cell and Mom's egg cell meet, but we know that's not the beginning of our lives. It's just the beginning of our lives on this earth. Our birth day is really just our welcome-to-earth day. It's one more marvelous step in Heavenly Father's great plan for the happiness and eternal progress of all of his children.

Questions and Answers for Older Children

Question: Why didn't God just give us bodies to start with?

Answer: Heavenly Father could have given his children physical bodies. We know this because he is the father of Jesus' physical body. But because God is immortal, which means he can never die, the bodies he would have provided for us would have been immortal from the beginning. We would have missed the experiences of being on earth that help us grow. Becoming like our Heavenly Parents requires much more than simply looking like them. By allowing moms and dads on earth to help provide bodies, everyone learns more. If we had been given bodies right from the start, without having to earn them through our righteousness, we may not have appreciated them or realized how valuable they are—kind of like getting a prize or an award you didn't have to earn or work for.

Question: Where do moms and dads keep the eggs and sperm?

Answer: Boys and girls are different—not so much in what they like to do or read or their sizes or shapes. The main difference is under their clothes, between their legs, where boys have a penis and girls have a vagina. Those different parts allow a boy and girl to make a baby together one day when they are married. Dad's sperm cells are made in two testicles, like large marbles, that hang under his penis in a sack of skin called the scrotum. Mom's egg cells are in her ovaries, which are inside her body, just above her vagina.

Question: How do the sperm cell and the egg cell come together?

Answer: When boys and girls grow up they sometimes fall in love and get married. When they want to have a family the husband fits his penis into his wife's vagina. This allows the sperm cell and egg cell to meet. It's called sex or making love. It feels good and helps the husband and wife feel close to each other to build a strong marriage that can welcome children. Couples don't have a baby every time they make love, but they can't have a baby without making love. Because sex is so important to Heavenly Father's plan, he has commanded us to never do this except when we are married. If men and women have sex without being married it is a serious sin—like stealing something that doesn't belong to you.

Question: Does the baby grow inside Mom's tummy?

Answer: Actually, the baby grows in a place a little below Mom's waist, called the uterus or womb. It is a little like a balloon that can stretch and expand as the baby gets bigger. Dads don't have a uterus, only moms. Helping babies grow is a special job Heavenly Father gives just to mothers.

Question: What about twins or triplets?

Answer: When twins or triplets are identical, it means that after the sperm and egg cells met they split and formed more than one body at the same time. When twins don't look alike it means two different sperm cells met up with two different egg cells and the babies just grew in the same space.

Question: How does the food get through a little tube?

Answer: You didn't eat the way you eat now, and you certainly couldn't order from a menu. Instead you shared your mom's food. Your mom would eat, and then her body would absorb the nutrients in the food. She would then pass those nutrients to you with her blood. That's also how you got your air, since you were surrounded by liquid and couldn't breath the way you do now. You got your oxygen through Mom's blood as it passed through the umbilical cord. That's why it's so important for moms to be healthy. If moms smoke, drink alcohol, or take illegal drugs while they are pregnant, they are sharing those harmful substances with their babies too.

Question: How do you hear the heart beat if the baby is inside the mom?

Answer: There are several different ways, but some parents get a sneak preview of their baby when the mom gets an ultrasound. It's a little like an x-ray machine that lets parents see a picture of the unborn baby and hear the heart beat. That's why some moms and dads know whether they are going to have a boy or girl even before the baby comes.

Question: How does Mom know when it's time to go to the hospital?

Answer: Her body tells her when it's time because the uterus begins to tighten up and then relax. She feels it. Sometimes the sack inside the uterus that holds the baby breaks, and the liquid that has surrounded the baby comes out of her vagina. If that happens, then Mom knows for sure it's time.

Question: Why do babies cry when they are born?

Answer: The birth process can be difficult for both moms and babies, but when babies cry it is usually because they are getting used to breathing and using their lungs. As babies grow they cry to communicate since they don't yet know how to talk. A cry can mean the baby is wet or tired or hungry. It's up to moms and dads to figure out what the cries mean.

Question: How does a baby learn to drink milk from Mom's breasts?

Answer: Even though babies are small and helpless, Heavenly Father sends them with a few special abilities right from the start. They all know how to suck automatically. They also know how to close their fingers around things. Next time you get a chance to hold a little baby, put your finger lightly in the baby's hand. Chances are the baby will grab hold of your finger and hold on tightly.

Question: What does it mean when someone is adopted?

Answer: Sometimes, a woman who has a baby cannot take care of that baby. Adoption makes it possible for a new mom and dad to love and care for the baby as if it had been born to them. They become the baby's parents, and the baby becomes their child. Parents in the Church can take their baby to the temple to be sealed to them forever. They may not be the baby's birth parents, but they are the baby's real parents and wil be throughout all time and eternity.

Question: How does a baby get its name?

Answer: Moms and dads get to choose the name for their baby. They know it will be an important part of their child's life from then on, so they usually spend a lot of time picking out just the right name. Names often have great meaning and parents choose them for important reasons. Latter-day Saints receive their names in a priesthood blessing that is usually given in front of all the members of their ward or branch. Worthy fathers, grandfathers, uncles, and other priesthood holders form a circle around the new baby, who is held gently in the center. In a prayer, the baby's name is given along with a blessing. Of course, the baby doesn't remember the words that are spoken, but God honors and fulfills the blessing. It is a special time for families and friends as they welcome the new arrival and surround the baby in a circle of love.

Question: Why do they call private parts *private*?

Answer: *Private* means personal, just for you. Private parts are places that are covered by your swimsuit. No one should touch your private parts. Other touching is good. Hugging, wrestling, shaking hands at church, or holding hands are great ways to let people know they matter to you and feel their love and acceptance in return. However, if someone touches your private parts, say, "Stop it!" and then tell your mom or dad. Sometimes you get curious about how other bodies look—especially underneath clothes. Some children play doctor and say, "I'll show you my private parts if you'll show me yours." Any place covered by a swimsuit should stay covered even when it's just a game. That's one way we show respect for our bodies and thank Heavenly Father for giving them to us.

Question: What if I still have questions this book didn't answer?

Answer: Ask Mom and Dad. They want to talk to you about these things and you can trust what they say. Sometimes they're not exactly sure how much to say, so your questions really help them out. Just remember to ask them when you're alone and not in the middle of a big group of people.

Brad Wilcox, author,
now and as a baby

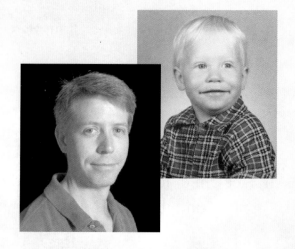

Brian Call, illustrator,
now and at age 1

About the Author and Illustrator

BRAD WILCOX was born in Provo, Utah, right on Christmas Day. His older brothers stayed with their grandma and were terribly worried that Santa would not find them. However, Santa came through, as he always does. Many years have passed since then, and Brad and his wife, Debi, have had four children of their own: Wendee, Russell, Whitney, and David. Brad teaches at Brigham Young University and has conducted maturation clinics for fifth and sixth graders throughout Utah. He finished this book just before leaving to serve as the president of the Chile Santiago East Mission.

BRIAN CALL has had a lifelong interest in drawing. He took his first art class at age nine and later went on to study art, graduating from Ricks College and Brigham Young University. After graduation he returned to his hometown of Idaho Falls, Idaho, where he began a career as an illustrator. He has done illustration work for many religious magazines across the nation, including the *Ensign* and the *Friend.* Brian is also the illustrator of the children's book *Sarah's Cloud.* He and his wife, Michelle, are the parents of five children: Brichelle, Natalie, Brittany, Bryant, and Kyle.

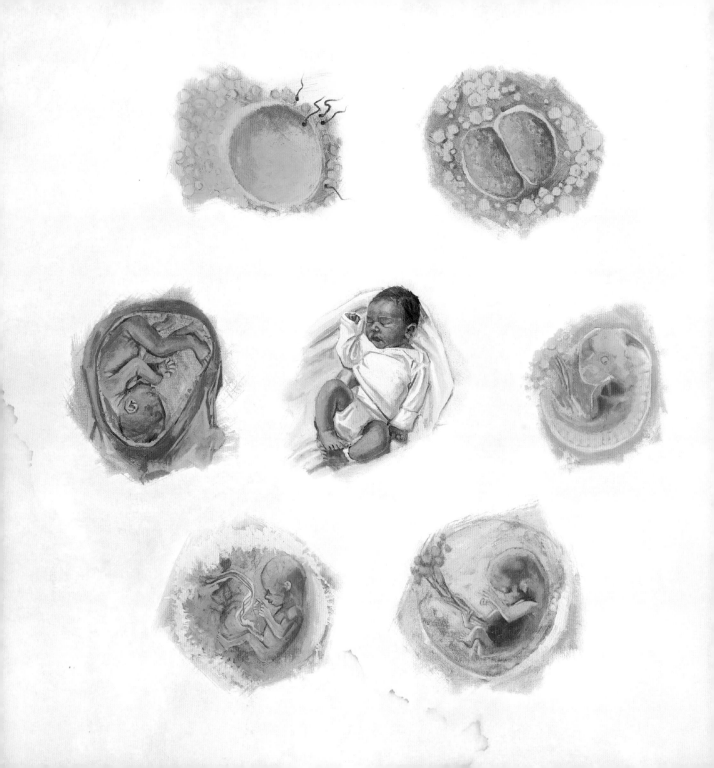